Give the gift that shows that special someone
how much you care!

Other *"Gifts of Hope™"* Series Selections

GIFT BOOK   🌸 *Gifts of Love™*

GIFT BOOK   🌸 *Gifts for the Family™*

GIFT BOOK   🌸 *Gifts for Life's Journey™*

🌸 *Perpetual Calendar*

🌸 *Blank Journal*

Available at fine bookstores nationwide
or call 1-800-242-5348

**RAINBOW
STUDIES
INTERNATIONAL**

Creating Colorful Treasures™

Some things have to be believed
to be seen.

Ralph Hodgson

Jesus told them, "This is the will of God,
that you BELIEVE in the one
he has sent."

John 6:29 TLB

Everything that we see
is a SHADOW
cast by that
which we do not see.

Martin Luther King, Jr.

There is one case
of death-bed repentance
recorded — the penitent thief —
that no one should despair;
and only one,
that no one should presume.

St. Augustine

Many persons who appear to repent
are like **sailors**
who throw their goods
overboard in a storm,
and wish for them again in a calm.

Mead

REPENTANCE

Repent! *Turn away from all your offenses;*

then sin will not be your downfall.

Rid yourselves of all the offenses

you have committed,

and get a new heart and a new spirit.

Ezekiel 18:30-31 NIV

To do it no more is the truest repentance.

Martin Luther

Now make confession
to the LORD,
the God of your fathers,
*and **do his will**.*

Ezra 10:11 NIV

CONFESSION

We're all proud of making

little *mistakes.*

It gives us the feeling

we don't make any

BIG *ones.*

Andrew A. Rooney

✝✝✝

I make mistakes; I'll be the second to admit it.

Jean Kerr

CONFESSION

Lord, when we are wrong,
make us willing to change.
And when we are right,
make us easy to live with.

Peter Marshall

When down in the mouth
remember Jonah —
he came out all right!

Thomas Edison

And now about fasting. When you fast,
declining your food for a spiritual purpose,
don't do it publicly, as the hypocrites do . . . .

Matthew 6:16 TJB

The best of all medicines
are resting and fasting.

Benjamin Franklin

God heals,

and the doctor takes the fee.

Benjamin Franklin

I treated him, God cured him.

Ambroise Paré

The report of his miracles
spread far beyond the borders of Galilee
so that sick folk
were soon coming to be healed
from as far away as Syria.
And whatever their illness and pain,
or if they were possessed by demons,
or were insane, or paralyzed —
he healed them all.

Matthew 4:24 TLB

HEALING

I'd rather give my life

than be afraid

to give it.

Lyndon B. Johnson

Give me **LIBERTY**
or give me death!

Patrick Henry

CONVICTION

Pain nourishes courage.

You can't be brave

if you've only had

WONDERFUL *things*

happen to you.

Mary Tyler Moore

COURAGE

COURAGE IS *resistance to fear,*
mastery of fear,
not absence of fear.

Mark Twain

The only thing we have to FEAR
is FEAR *itself.*

Franklin D. Roosevelt

He who loses wealth loses much;
he who loses a friend loses more;
but he that loses his courage
loses all.

Miguel de Cervantes

Cowards die many times

before their death;

The **valiant** *never taste*

of death but once.

William Shakespeare

COURAGE

Often the test of courage

is not to die

but to live.

Vittorio Alfieri

COURAGE

COURAGE

is not the towering oak

that sees storms come and go;

it is the fragile blossom

that opens in the snow.

Alice Mackenzie Swaim

COURAGE

is grace

under

pressure.

Ernest Hemingway

I have found the perfect antidote for fear.
Whenever it sticks up its ugly face
I clobber it with prayer . . . .

Dale Evans Rogers

I've learned to admit it when I'm scared
because it takes courage to know
when you ought to be afraid.

James A. Michener

PRAYER & COURAGE

Have I not commanded you?

Be strong *and courageous.*

Do not be terrified; do not be discouraged,

for the LORD your God will be with you

wherever you go.

Joshua 1:9 NIV

COURAGE

In matters of style, swim with the current;
in matters of principle, **stand** *like a rock.*

Thomas Jefferson

Right *is right, even if everyone is against it,*
and **wrong** *is wrong, even if everyone is for it.*

William Penn

Why is it the **ship** *beats the waves*
when the waves are so many and the ship is one?
The reason is that ship has a PURPOSE.

Winston Churchill

CONVICTION

One person with

a belief

is equal to a force of 99

who only have

interest.

John Stuart Mill

It's easy to make a *buck*.

It's a lot tougher

to make a *difference*.

Tom Brokaw

CONVICTION

A man who wants
to **lead**
the orchestra
must turn his back
on the crowd.

Anonymous

My mother said to me,
"If you become a soldier you'll be a general;
if you become a monk you'll end up as the pope."
Instead, I became a painter
and wound up as Picasso.

Pablo Picasso

We are all worms,
but I do believe
I am a
glowworm.

Winston Churchill

Some people grumble
because roses have thorns.
*I am **thankful** that thorns have roses.*

Karr

When you say a situation

or a person is HOPELESS,

you are slamming the door

in the face of God.

Charles L. Allen

When somebody tells you

nothing is impossible,

ask him to dribble

a football.

Anonymous

We're going to get in
two hours
of good practice
even if it takes
six hours.

Lou Holtz

CONVICTION

I wouldn't ever set out
*to hurt anybody **deliberately***
unless it was, you know, important —
like a league **game** *or something.*

Dick Butkus

CONVICTION

When I was in the batter's box,
I felt sorry for the pitcher.

Roger Hornsby

If I only had a little HUMILITY
I would be perfect.

Ted Turner

It ain't

over

till it's

over.

Lawrence "Yogi" Berra

I've never LOST a game
in my life.
Once in a while,
time ran out on me.

Bobby Layne

WINNING

isn't everything,
but it beats anything
that comes in second.

Paul "Bear" Bryant

If you don't
have CONFIDENCE,
you'll always
find a way
not to WIN.

Carl Lewis

Heads I win,
tails you lose.

Anonymous

*There's no
substitute
for guts.*

Paul "Bear" Bryant

COURAGE

Shoot *for the moon.*

Even if you miss it

you will **land** *among the stars.*

Les Brown

*Don't be afraid
to take big steps.
You can't cross a chasm
in two small jumps.*

David Lloyd George

No bird SOARS
too HIGH *if he soars*
with his own wings.

William Blake

Ah, but a man's reach
should exceed his grasp,
Or what's a heaven for.

Robert Browning

The ripest peach
is highest
on the tree.

James Whitcomb Riley

CONVICTION

I can do

all things

through Christ

which strengtheneth me.

Philippians 4:13 KJV

I tell you the truth,
if you have FAITH as small as
a mustard seed, you can say to this
MOUNTAIN,
"Move from here to there"
and it will move. Nothing will be
impossible for you.

Matthew 17:20 NIV

FAITH

When
we *do*
what we
can,
God *will do*
what we
can't.

Anonymous

MIRACLES

Just pray for a tough hide

and

a tender heart.

Ruth Bell Graham

Do not pray for easy lives;
pray to be stronger men!
Do not pray for tasks
equal to your powers,
pray for powers
equal to your tasks . . . .

Phillips Brooks

PRAYER

Prayer does not equip us

for greater works —

PRAYER *is*

the greater work.

Oswald Chambers

Very early in the morning, while it was still dark,
Jesus got up, left the house and went off
to a SOLITARY *place,*
where he prayed.

Mark 1:35 NIV

I have been driven many times to my knees
by the overwhelming **conviction**
that I had nowhere else to go.

Abraham Lincoln

And Satan trembles when he sees
The weakest SAINT *upon his knees.*

William Cowper

Oh, Adam was a gardener,

and God who made him sees

That half a proper gardener's work

is done upon his knees.

Rudyard Kipling

PRAYER

THE LORD'S PRAYER

is not, as some fancy,

the easiest, the most natural

of all devout utterances.

It may be committed

to memory quickly, but it is

slowly learned by heart.

John F. D. Maurice

PRAYER

If you don't have faith,
pray anyway.
*If you don't understand
or believe the words you're saying,*
pray anyway.
*Prayer can start faith,
particularly if you pray aloud.
And even the most imperfect prayer
is an attempt to reach God.*

Cary Grant

Groanings which cannot

be uttered are often

PRAYERS

which cannot

be refused.

Charles Spurgeon

In prayer
it is better to have
a HEART
without words
than words
without a
HEART

John Bunyan

Prayer is not overcoming
God's reluctance,
it is laying hold
of His highest willingness.

R. C. Trench

More things are wrought by

PRAYER

than this WORLD

dreams of.

Alfred, Lord Tennyson

Trust *in God —*

but tie your camel tight.

Persian Proverb

Christians and camels
receive their burdens kneeling.

Ambrose Bierce

Any concern too small

to be turned into a

PRAYER

is too small to be

made into a burden.

Corrie ten Boom

PRAYER

Let my **HEART**

be broken by the things

that break

the **HEART** *of God.*

Bob Pierce

We must accept finite disappointment,
but we must never lose infinite hope.

Martin Luther King, Jr.

If it were not for hopes, the heart would break.

Thomas Fuller

HOPE is the best part

of our riches. —

What sufficeth it that we have

the wealth of the Indies

in our pockets, if we have not

the HOPE of heaven

in our souls?

Bovee

You cannot put a great hope
into a small soul.

J. L. Jones

To **EAT** *bread*

without **HOPE** *is still slowly*

to **STARVE** *to death.*

Pearl S. Buck

The message
of *DAWN*
is hope.

Winston Churchill

Let us **HOLD** *unswervingly to the hope we profess,
for he who promised is faithful.*

Hebrews 10:23 NIV

*I believe the promises of God
enough to venture an eternity on them.*

G. Campbell Morgan

And when the centurion,
who stood there in front of Jesus,
heard his cry and saw
how he died, he said,
"Surely this man was
the Son of God!"

Mark 15:39 *NIV*

CONVICTION

✝✝✝

The object of your FAITH

must be Christ.

Not FAITH in ritual,

not FAITH in sacrifices,

not FAITH in morals,

not FAITH in yourself —

not FAITH in anything but CHRIST!

Billy Graham

Sorrow
looks
back,

worry
looks
around,

faith
looks
up.

Anonymous

FAITH *is*

a refusal

to PANIC.

D. Martyn Lloyd-Jones

FAITH

Fear
knocked
at the door.
Faith
answered.
No one
was there.

Anonymous

The *"FAITH"* Themes

FAITH ~ PRAYER ~ MIRACLES

COURAGE ~ CONFESSION

REPENTANCE ~ FASTING

HEALING ~ HOPE ~ CONFIDENCE

CONVICTION ~ BELIEF

God and I can do It!

Gifts of Faith™

"Gifts of Hope™*" Series*

Compiled by Billy & Janice Hughey

RAINBOW
STUDIES
INTERNATIONAL

Creating Colorful Treasures™